mahogany

also by erica lewis

mary wants to be a superwoman (2017)

daryl hall is my boyfriend (2015)

murmur in the inventory (2013)

camera obscura (2010)

mahogany

erica lewis

Wesleyan University Press

Middletown, Connecticut

Wesleyan University Press
Middletown CT 06459
www.wesleyan.edu/wespress
2023 © erica lewis
Manufactured in the United States of America
Designed by Jessy Yohn
Typeset in Palatino® by Linotype

Library of Congress Cataloging-in-Publication Data

Names: Lewis, Erica, author.
Title: Mahogany / Erica Lewis.
Description: First edition. | Middletown, Connecticut: Wesleyan
University Press, 2023. | Series: Wesleyan poetry | "The third book
in a trilogy." | Summary: "The third book in a trilogy revising the
confessional, mahogany uses the music of Diana Ross as an emotive/
sonic echo into which the poet sings the realities of being a grown,
Black woman, losing everyone you ever loved, and still surviving,
finding your calling and learning to love your beautiful, broken
self"—Provided by publisher.
Identifiers: LCCN 2023012277 (print) | LCCN 2023012278 (ebook) |
ISBN 9780819500762 (Hardcover) | ISBN 9780819500779 (Paperback)
| ISBN 9780819500786 (Ebook)
Subjects: BISAC: POETRY / Subjects & Themes / General | POETRY
/ Subjects & Themes / Family | LCGFT: Poetry.
Classification: LCC PS3612.E9645 M35 2023 (print) | LCC PS3612.
E9645 (ebook) | DDC 811/.6—dc23/eng/20230421
LC record available at https://lccn.loc.gov/2023012277
LC ebook record available at https://lccn.loc.gov/2023012278

for mary

my only sunshine

It took many years of vomiting up
All the filth I'd been taught
About myself, and half-believed,
Before I was able to walk on the earth
As though I had a right to be here

— James Baldwin, *The Price of the Ticket*

I fell apart many times.
So.
What does that say about me,
Besides I live through wars.

— Nayyirah Waheed, *Salt*

You are my sunshine
My only sunshine

—"You Are My Sunshine," performed by The Pine Ridge Boys (1939)

contents

// teak

// litmus

// mahogany

first, i must accept me.

// teak

*baby, baby**

kiss my lips
ain't no harm
to moan
rhythm
and change
of rhythm
gave you my life
transmissions
to my white blood
some faraway
satellite
six-foot hole
inside my chest
cobalt ribs
as intimate
whisper
the truth is
i see you
i see you
and god grew
tired of us
fucking
on the ghost
of the truth

* *"where did our love go"*

*like you do**

this is the year
of hibernation
drunk deep
from the light
you are my life
sometimes
be in love
with what was
separate
the lord's
prayer
april is a blur
white noise
for sleep
or how i express
that love
towards you
be an ocean
and a stone
someone's child
formed
in the ancient
slip away
well-guarded
bullshit
drive down
the western coast
the old testament
the real thing is
you must
know by now
i will love you
to the motherfucking end

*"baby love"

*crying baby**

tennessee whiskey
slave narrative
life goes on
ladybug
whiting out
all the details
accepting
their inadequacy
the people
who passed on
their genetic
material to you
say my grace
so i show up
and surrender
crawl into
the gigantic arms
of my ancestors
and hammock-rest
in them
these hands
my hands now
in a large
beautiful garden
cotton
don't have no heroes
and what we have
is half the story
memory of house
house of sleep patterns
bring me something
don't just take
something from me
our beds are made
in the distance
a black bench post
if you will stay
i will stay here too

* *"come see about me"*

*think it over**

after the fall of rome
isn't that exactly
how it is sometimes
how dreams be
the color
before the sun
when the garden
was an eden
gloss of bees
the homesman
some kind of beautiful
sex money happiness goals
what craves to be done
what's left behind
we are the sweet ok
burden in time
world
be a mirror
all the blessing
i need
when our pride
was low
all this earth
had to be
removed
face to face
blended babies
our little house
those million hearts
right back at you

*so satisfied**

walk the moon
stardust rain
drops in a jar
the way you sing to me
the source considered
we changed the world
said this is a love
and this is a love
that we won't get right
where i see my change
see my child
alone in the blind
grass of my youth
birth
death
dreams
that feeling
of laying down
on sweltering
concrete
and wild
blood orchids
imagine the fairies
we learn it slow
fake glow
soft inheritance
but i want it
to be good
i want it
to be so good
it kills me

* *"back in my arms again"*

fallout
is a time of rituals
is opus
is cut-glass
one more year
and then
you'll be happy
one more year
we worked
in the sugar fields
called it an omen
had the funeral
for our white people
problems
five-minute rule
hung
like the moon
we thought the same
silly way
like fuck
the river inside
where's my god
and where's my money
in memory of all
the black people
and holes
that are hard
to explain
keeping the sun
up off our bones
shitting beliefs
waiting
for the afterglow

*my mind and soul**   *for sueyeun juliette lee*

i wish i could live
in a perfect world
in the jungle
and run free
with the animals
covered in crazy
rays of hope
have presence
in the belly
of bad situations
love
when i comfortably can
when do you stop
counting
beneath the surface
anniversary of her death
anniversary of his death
trajectories
a pot to piss in
that pain we all
rush towards
everything
in a sweet time
independent hustle
deep down low
in the water well
my body
quiet inside
my body
every kingdom
was recorded
getting by
on arrogant
details of loss
maybe i'm not here
to be a superstar
but for some
soft nameless joy
am resurrected
in a room
in a space

that isn't mine
i remember
i remember
i remember
i forgive
i haven't danced
this hard
outside
my living
room
since forever

poetry in the heart-stopping
my body
this last winter
flying higher
than a georgia pine
thankful
for all the dead people
because at least they tried
our skin
was a terrible thing
to live in
paint your face
you have taken
my life
with my arms
behind my back
and now
i will only ever
love you
with my arms
behind my back
sometimes
we need to burn
the whole
fucking house down
to get at the truth
maybe you need
to do more
of the burning
rather than having
others set little fires
all over you
rings
for every finger
are hardly trees
all of this
has passed
between us
because i am
so full of grief
but you

you will find
a window
you will find
a flame
fall into the river
fall into the river
and just keep on
swimming

*mama can't help me**   *for marthe reed*

21st century medicine show
paint my body gold
the end of the world
is always pretty
indifferent
to our emotions
early fragments
and bamboo
flourishing
in extreme conditions
our skin
is a terrible thing
to live in
great fantasies
of our own reliance
allman by way
of kentucky
coal mines
salvaging
this part of my life
that isn't my life
we sang
the most
heart wrenching songs
when they didn't
add up
to anything
but your pale
pink heart
in the soil
in the water
in the air
trail of red dirt
california
when you lose
track of time
hunger, strength
drops of blood
resemble
blackfoot
inclusions

so you will
get through this
and we will burn
our former sorrows
with the black coal
of wisdom
and get high
off your possessions
great spirit
on my tongue
your fierce
is just under
your skin

*give and take**

ancient sunday
quitters raga
they can't teach
what they can't prove
i should write a book
about wearing white
and tusk fulfillment
how they make
crystals
and shit in general
our endless inclusions
got my hands on a clip
saw blood
and a bit of it was mine
we going to war
so show me how
when black children
are sad
it's about letting go
of top-down
narratives
and letting the hive
take control
set the world on fire
from the radiance
of an orange tree
world be a mirror
whiting out
all the details
as though it were
an inside fucking joke
in five-minute
increments
between myself
and the universe
who am i to you
sometimes
that is all
the blessing i need
to burn it all down
when b.b. passed away

i kind of woke up and said
love is deep shit
now we can go out
and destroy
the universe

the discipline
of painting white
the limitations
of dancing horses
how a whole city
wants to hurt you
silent passage
understated
desire system
just sitting
on my hands
listen
moth wind
what happens
when you replace
your eyes
your face
your heart
i call it
"the key of e means
everything will be alright"
i am more fearless now
these are my hands now
i believe the shit we say
the aforementioned
liquor store oreos
if the journey
came this way
then it's my pain
i bet on diamonds
and the starry night
grieve for the lost
places in your life
when you dream
of childhood
somebody
always wearing black
sentiment
makes you want
to do right
shatter a little bit

to survive
in the long run
when you lose
track of time
hunger, strength
please
calm me of myself
the bay of fires
we get old
we get faithful
we get tired
but world
we gone
be alright

you can always come back to the tribe
history of touches
began with bleakness
black oxidized circle
on blindness
that time we were mirages
grabbed our eyes
our elsewhere music
moon rang like a bell
prelude
used morse code
another's teeth is your luck
wish upon wolves
call yourself something wild
why the mountains are black
scarecrow figures getting crucified
close your eyes and nod off
we jog, we sprint, we dance
we set our intention
carry my roots with me
am the center of a circle of pain

*i had no name**

music arrived at home
how can i right
my wrongs
quit running to jesus
when the pain
becomes exotic
another mountain
growing up
dreams
turning inside out
like all the planes
we flew
the sweetness
of a honeycomb tree
my body
spinning around
in white water
and the kids got cokes
and chocolate bars
and we're supposed
to forget
four hundred years
of throw us a bone
and dig out the truth
cowman oxfords
mixing fire with fire
they let us sing
and dance
and smile
but took us
from our land
by our teeth
bones
marrow
and i'm pretty
messed up
all the time
over liquor stores
and old school jams
our history
is one of the greatest

crimes
but i feel love
for you right now
like quartz
laid down
in bands
we've died
in the wrong order
so nothing real
can be threatened

"love child"

*yes, i will**

atmospheric rivers
call me by my real name
like malcolm
in mecca in '65
aiming too high
wanting too much
resurrecting images
of forefathers
left limp
like ali over liston
i don't know
where the recent
dead have gone
but i hope
wherever it is
god keeps
a better eye
on their sparrows
let me cover
your shit
in glitter
our love
and grief
its own solace
nature of this life
is its systemic
inevitability
a kind of faith
and rhetoric
we know
as we have
known nothing
i can't remember
the last time
something wasn't
going to shit
staggered
that it did not
flood
black triangles
in a red field

rosewood casket
hold your breath
every time
break everything
you are
gravity seems
a mistake
show me a history
and i'll start
you owe yourself
the love
you so freely give
to other people

*as there are stars above**

april is a tired month
of true conviction
crisis
in negro leadership
black neon
break everything you are
to give your grief some space
nothing has changed
the circumstances
of existing
it's your weakness
that they want
has caused
my sorrow
laid down
my powerful
because i have stolen
and so have you
because it be
a new world
with an entirely
different taste
to think
of our hearts
as value
question desire
and life's priorities
that strange link
between quiet and empathy
if we could dance
like fire
if two flames go out
the world is ready
to sell our suffering
my only child
to the spot
where we were
burned
touch that bit
of ground
we are the ones

we've been
waiting for
future stuck
inside our throats
flood dollar
for every dream
and empire built
in the shade of trees
i remember the day
whitney houston died
didn't we all just break
didn't we all just break
each other's hearts

"someday we'll be together"

*ain't no river**

house is a gauntlet
journey
from the panther's mouth
you do see a pattern, right
when we was
washed up
along the sea
beestung lips
teak
driftwood
drag your name
as if your name
is not our name
being forever on the verge
i cannot reimagine our lives
the parts we once abandoned
drinking orange crush
straight
from the bottle
my crazy ass
brother
i must hope
that wisdom
is not a word
of slander
we fake memories
screw current age
to the sticking place
who was also my monster
my tongue
until i choke
let the damn water be
the bomb
& altogether beautiful
everything
that is burning down
the metallic abyss
the god dream
around my neck
sometimes i wear
all my chains

at once
walk through the fire
and never shed
the heat

"ain't no mountain high enough"

*make this world**

to change birds
all this history
you have in your life
we are surrounded
by the fucking wolves
sometimes
take off our clothes
to find the truth
the start of our safe dream
where shawls have been used
in prayer preserved
like angel cake
rituals for centuries
if i had money
i'd have a baby
move to la
or tennessee
cherry red arcadia
written
in my native tongue
black mountain
mineral love
the hard work is done
i'll take it from here
hold my liquor
like the saints do
our love in cold blood
more than monument
or tissue
your mama
she ain't never
going to be the same
either i survive
or cradle the earth
kick these rocks
in the river
in the river
be a vessel

// litmus

at last i taste the honey*

post pop depression
pulls me back from words
all i can think of
is that this is the year
we lost everything
of the fire monkey
and radical change
elegies to prince
in the river blood
i have hardened
at least in some ways
like a hummingbird
like an hourglass
too good
for the chitlin circuit
come home
and heal yourself
i can feel our fire
as we all die
of thirst

* *"now that there's you"*

*baby, don't you know**

moonshine
on the northside
we all talkin
about lemonade
to mend things
moving forward
smoked everything
except our shoes
an elephant on this soft
this little gravestone
egyptian revival gold
like where is my beautiful life
and all the beauty
fucking to formation
grinding
until it smells like fire
until fingers bow down
to invaluable weakness
to knees
and dark necessities
and how you gone live with yourself
makes you want
to do right
in spite of the debris
the only vehicle
from point a
to point b
leaf and tea
your thighs
and sentiment
so tired
of being attracted
to the damage
this is the way
to remember
songs the body
burned away
i can see your mother
in your eyes
whatever it takes
to get from there
to here

"something on my mind"

nefertiti meant "the beautiful
(or perfect) woman has come"
i am afraid to be loved
the way i really want
to be loved
to be beautiful
when our museum
is still
a hypothetical space
that was never there
we ask for permission
where we only have
ourselves as company
i have ativan so
#prescriptiondrugsforthewin
in the first place
mid century ankh
atlas shrugged
the weight of the world
so why do you hold on to so much
this is mental illness
jesus at the day spa
the tiredness of not
having the ability to say
i'm not here for america
i love this book as i love erica
it's time for us to go
back to that tradition
to walk in the rain
or sit in the sunshine
i am sitting in my car
in the grocery store parking lot
listening to lionel ritchie on the PA
so emotionally exhausted
i can't move
it's like some sad
wes anderson outtake
that wound up
on the cutting room floor
the cincinnati cut
african tribal fetish bone

brass god face
we crumble
fetched in glass
and later on
when it gets dark
we go home
for a thousand years
of sleep

*i'm like a woman who once knew splendor**

sometimes i feel like the pink panther
all naked and pink
lost in the morass of
do the best you can today
and nigga heal thy self
our end of winter
spirits break
like old tibetan snow
i remember
you was conflicted
and i found myself alone
here on my ancient hurt
the disquieting hum
of living history
dear god, please
put my head above my heart
we can only be together
if the stories are told
plain face
same instrument
just a couple of coke bottles
full of gasoline
like god and rain
is a waste of time
my mother used to clean houses
as a child
some days i can barely
get out of bed
in my mind
she's like diana ross
scrubbing the white lady's stairs
in *lady sings the blues*
except prettier
and with green eyes
i've just been living
off of cough drops
and water and anger
just sitting in the whole foods
parking lot eating pineapple
i am literally
the definition of "hot mess"

pain changes everything
somebody come
and pick up
my limp body
off the ground
i am dying
a slow ohio death
we miss you starman
it's our first sunrise of the burn

*the sky to shelter me**

theremin dreams
places of your body
where my hands
have been
bone of my bones
every kind of incense tree
there is something
so powerful and real
about being able to hold
presence despite
woundedness
in this world
if love be your saint
bless them
in their place of need
cause we both
died in the fire
seriously
think of ways
to gradually return
to the world
but i am covered
in fat and bruises
resinous heartwood
oud
speak of the devil
of doing or not doing
the wrong thing
loneliness
that we cling to
being still
losing
and getting lost
letting go
of what wants to be kept
and muhammad ali is dead
and we are dead, too
impostors
in this country you know
years of our ribbed cage
dreaming and waking

running together
i am dying
a slow ohio death
repeat after me:
i am the greatest
i am a robot
made of bones
hurl my fuck screams
to heaven
the jungle is the only way out

*it ain't enough**   *for amanda ackerman*

summer was always ours
spectrums of the black
stories we tell
pinks and greens
nourishing your heart
you need more
yellows and golds, too
a complicated sunburn
you can't trust
your own mind
you thought
you been carrying
race, power, tradition
but the land here
the rain here
feels soft
shows you
instantly
when you fall
self-made medicine
wind in your fox fur
maybe today is the day
i will cry for no reason
have sex to nourish
my equilibrium
gospel shoes
where you emerge
why not believe
in the superstar
that small bit of melt
my child to live her life
my child to take her life
get a tequila
and share
our open wounds
i remember my dream now
an indian woman pouring
oil onto my hair
combing through it
do you really love that man
afraid of water

afraid of the sky
a fool is an idea
an idea improvised
but your heart
is intact
your heart
is intact

*pray for the lonely**   *for brett price*

litmus test
the songs you need in your life
noise and beauty
we all the light
are interdependent
got scars
from the life before
got scars before my life
in violet pouches
coughing up blood
ability
to go there
and here
sacrifice
the burning bush
house looking like
grey gardens
love with
some other dude
all the poets
treat you bad
for your own good
if i insist on analogies
the gay bar using me too
but i need my eighteen karat jesus
i know sex that tastes like endings
that shit almost got me
thrown down
two flights of stairs
declaration
or deliverance
get me something sweet
to turn is a type of magic
we swallow ourselves again
spend our days
lighting matches
to the eastern spirit
in that very darkness
like your hair could be tamed
into this thing of bridges
like the drowned tread water

the way true love begins
only the living
need each other

*the signs of misery**

what gives you life
when i die
i will sail
to my ancestors
pocket full of lemons
for my lemonade
water bless myself
around the facts
trying to claim
my miraculous
i don't know any woman
in my family
that did something
just for themselves
we were always
towing people
out of slavery
out of harm's way
teaching them
to swim
in the gusset blues
some people break
their very selves
and some people
just stay broken
hole in my belly
keeps growing
still got to wake up
and be someone
dry my eyes
using another method
mercy
in their perfume
sex as radical self care
i want to learn to give
i want to learn
to give and receive
drained the spirits
from the jar
and brushed my teeth
we are aligned

you are just late for dinner
to have shaped a history
we beautiful
beautiful people
who thunderdomed
for this spot
let it bleed
black medicine
black so black
it's black
to the core

*we had yesterday**

the dark history of servitude
it is an act of terrorism
not to recognize one's self
blood as feral fluid
there are no fists
in the air this time
everybody want that dollar
got yo bougie
in my back pocket bitch
cotton club days
and futures we own
feeling fucked up
we abandoned detroit
it became too black
until the blood
went to our heads
and we had to stop
in the house of the lord
all that's wrong with me
is wrong with you
big love
but they took
our diamonds
our gold
even our people
robbed us
by convincing us
it was never ours
this radically altering self
fucking a stranger
in a alabama hotel room
need to rise up
like crops
we wear about ourselves
these costumes
our november collection
when you are rammed
with a rod through your core
you get up
learn what it means
to live in a world

where you can be
ripped apart
from the inside
our spiritual garments
so wounded
no bones in your body are dry
keep dying in little ways
but i love you
beyond any love
we have not drowned
in the river
for we are the sea

*ain't that easy**

when i look at my life
i feel like bursting into tears
marriage
and mental illness
vintage washed
michael jackson graphic
spiritual disco grieving ritual
sell your body
to your horse-eyed past
little fictions
somebody got to sing
and somebody
got to play the squaw
last time i saw him
last time i saw my honey
buried your dead
lack of afro
exit wounds
cut off whole limbs
of generational desire
the death of cleopatra
hell or high water
get some fucking
love in your life girl
ghost chant
you've got to die
if you want to live
amidst and against
the things we are
rubbed into the cloth
wrapped around their faces
now white men
are black men too
the ways
we can't say no
i call you queen
not as a term of endearment
but as a reminder
our histories meet
on the inside
we all be black moses

slave for the river
same river twice
sometimes
have to emphasize
the brown part
hey there beautiful brown girl
we don't usually change
until things are so painful
that we must

*all i feel is strong**

bees are often the answer
volunteered slavery
look good
against the yellow
luxury seed
trap of visibility
we ain't feeling time
forever swag
your pride
be your motherfuckin prison
and prison be a place
impossible
to explain
niggas need to live
like it was the '70s
i rode this land way back when
the loom and the pimp
be a national mood
you are body diver witness
america is a tire fire, ya'll
my new home
a land of monsters
of welcome
to your paradise
got to save
something for yourself
weapon of personal truth
the tip of the iceberg
and you understand the iceberg
tap the tree
and the syrup come out
grounded in artifice
head in a noose
we are still in debt
to our obscenities
still i am pharaoh
dressed in my best
attempt to unhitch love
from nostalgia
skin be blue-black
but i believe in this moment

and consensual drowning
water taking in a lover
or how we die weak
from indigo
wrapped around our faces
from a reason
rubbed into cloths
gave the world
my blood last night
gave the world
my love last night

custom made
dream instruments
the dailiness
of finding that joy
babylon
was once great too
diamonds dancing
on the rubies
all my cherokee
undertones
look at the fucking sun
you tear the clothes
instead of tearing
your body
embrace
the mess of yourself
i am bleeding moonlight
i just want
a whiskey and a man
i just want to have
impossibly
beautiful babies
snake sheds its skin
so we can shed our illusions
come back
to see things
we thought
we understood
you see
no one said "us"
that love you're in
is all fucked up
disco balled my kitchen
disco balled my life
sometimes
god's blessings
are not in what he gives
but what he takes away
stop trying
to pick up
what god told you

to put down
we ran in the open
now we know
what's in the wild
all the plants
growing
through concrete
gave you my song
a long time ago
so you be
beautiful now
not broken

to keep my self respect *   *for megan kaminski*

fuck me like a rockstar
controlled burn
i am imagining
the earth moving
unconditionally
for us
occasional lovers
my mama made greens
in anticipation
of my youth
the ancient
and reimagined woman
i'm looking forward
to showing you
around the prairie
we can talk more
in the beautiful
prairie light
battle rhyme
hymn book
this is hard but true
a lot of what weighs
us down isn't ours
to carry
saltwater gloss
soft cheetah
feather spiral
it's like all of a sudden
people realized
"she's mad"
like it was so
hidden before
beyoncé said
drink this lemonade
if we love
we will be replaced
smudge feathers
seed inside seem
so slow to grow
we will walk
and see the buffalo

be a badass
love beam
i'll save you a spot
no problem at all

*love me**

dear grace jones
why did your blood stop
singing its sweet song
i know this hurts
you have not now
nor ever been
a citizen
of the united states
welcome to the party
let's party like the '70s
our external wars
in the black power sense
sitting there reciting
your own
damn worth
i would rather die
penniless and naked
in the jungle
how all of a sudden
we are black
since *black panther* came out
shoutout to your money
and al green though
sugar and grits
the end
of my ability
to handle
my own suffering
i'm pretty sure
that toni morrison quote
was not penned
as a casual invitation
for whiteness
to explain itself
i don't need anyone else
fucking up
my goddamn heart
you mean the horrible
things you want
or your personal reality
spirit choker

i stand on these
the historically fractured
what is right
in front of you
this recording
is so beautiful
thank you for sharing it
i hope you are well
that the disciples of sun ra
blew your mind
i just need
some good dick and advice
to once again
become
a thing that feels

this is where it all began
the restless ones in black and blue
gave up his children
to spare their lives
to spare my life
his children sold
what good is knowing
the language
songs the body
burned away
hooded cotton parade
human condition
i am still bleeding moonlight
native american values
with white people problems
went through the words
in the harm jar today
too many people
caught
in too many
floods
america
is a motherfucker
to us
mahogany recovered
ghosts that you need
and mama says this is deep
the two feathers
being brought to you
but this is life i say
fire at the teepee tonight
we need drums for dreaming
the ghost dance
in defense of being ourselves
how old is beautiful
fairy godchile
she says the word "rose"
before every sentence
she speaks
she likes that word best today
that is a good way to see the world

close the circle
to the river, baby
wish we could all learn
to say "rose" before we speak

'80s pop was so glamorous
and heartbroken
i am collapsing slowly
trying to drink myself
to kingdom come
some glamorous
and heartbroken
get drunk
be famous
ocean death
the disconnect
between success
and true happiness
small moments
of messy, open love
my loneliness
jesus will kill you
and won't let you bleed out
into a mug
of elegant backfires
today i climbed
the biggest mountain
i've ever seen
there are a lot
of really basic girls here
they kind of look like the '90s
but unironically
i refuse to spend
the second half of my life
in ruins
reminded
of this ride
called american guilt
every caged bird want to fly
what up, bed-stuy
i've decided not
to let anyone
kill me again
when i die
i hope to god
i get to ride

in the sky
like johnny cash
in a big black cadillac
what up, bed-stuy
all dreamy orange
like children's aspirin
wish we could just
sit on the stoop
and smoke
and watch *broad city*
you know
forever

i don't want to live*

do you
love yourself
we must travel
in the direction
of our fear
and now the frontier is gone
i need to start
a garden of urgency
to capture
the vanishing race
already confined
to reservations
the historically fractured
home is not where
you were born
what good is knowing
the language
give me the gospel
the jukebox
romanticized notion
informed by the shitstorm
let's make rainbows
let's make decisions
be both hellfire
and holy water
a new aesthetic
for racial statement
countee cullen
on these i stand
like everything
been leading
up to now and now
today is the day
to get your life right
vintage cock inlay
things we found
in the holes
of the newly dead
home is where
all your attempts
to escape cease

blue disco bloom
one way or another
we all get institutionalized
the lord is my shepherd
i shall not want
for the appearance
of these teeth
i would rather die
penniless
and naked
in the jungle
in the jungle
how lovely i am

*never measure love by time**

sunday is for the children
interrogating
how i actually show up
for myself in this world
guilt and grief
are just a part of you now
sweet figs rotting
in the damp soil
living out of alignment
is the new bleeding
we just pretend
we want more freedom
run a marathon
because that is
so much easier
than resting
aesop resurrection
aretha is dead
and i just can't
get that donnie hathaway
song out of my head
like i can't be black
without a history
of systematic oppression
prayer boxes
and worry beads
our two selves
clinging
like love
i know we last
i know our bleeding
stops
to think beyond the wound
is a healing
that can't happen
yet
jesus put it this way:
i am the voice
of silence
and false alarms
black man get yo money

go to a new city
wear some new clothes
wake up at different times
and allow
all the things
that already want to come
into your life
to be real
in the chain
of open sea
if love is the new money
this is your compass
this is america
i hope the wound
is small and heals
quickly

there are things that should be said
i have felt
like a firehouse
it is a serious thing
to be alive
on this flesh
burning morning
in this broken ass
world
electric sky church
jimi i been thinking about you
and your nappy head
the fresh air
inhaled
after a summer
of drowning
i sleep
but choose the irrevocably
broken image
of my old boss
supervising everything i do
my father person
shaking his head
the old love of my life
turning me away
but always saying
i love you
but you never did
in this STAYHOME
i find me one more time
there are some moments
when i'm happy
but i know nothing
about fits of joy
welcome to the new ok
art deco bronze jesus
fun like ice cream
our common humanity
so very young
in this week of familiar pain
we are jealous of what

we fear we cannot
give to ourselves
yesterday's gesture
is tomorrow's
revolution
the joy
we think
we do not
deserve
without you
i get kind of lost
in the world
and need reminders
scream so loud
i can taste
my entire life
i mean i love you
but you always
want too much

abundance of light*

plain face
same instrument
the holy prophet
referred to agarwood
as a distinct item
found in paradise
how the heartbreak
i've gone through
recently also clouds
my way of seeing the world
i save me for a parable
our parents die
and this is how
we get our houses
and here i am
grieving, on edge
trying to make sure
you don't think
i am making
some sort of pass at you
it is the year of being
silent
a spiritual illness
she must cure herself
my great aunt chris
introduced me
to the rolling stones
when i was three
let me jump on her bed
to "miss you"
sometimes
i want to say to myself
i won't miss you child
i grew up watching
uncertainties
the price is right
press your luck
tic tac dough
and what's my line
that's still my favorite
everybody that raised me

is dead
i feel as uncertain
about everything
now as i did back then
i am once again reduced
to my condolences
george floyd
a metaphor for all these things
i don't know how
to talk
to anyone
who is not
myself
i am enjoying
how the wreckage
can take you home

// mahogany

*my spirit was free**

it is the year of return
to open the wounds
where there are no songs
but nigga heal thy self
summer was trash
cotton vintage
white grinding
and freshly washed sheets
misread "grateful" as "chateau"
the ghost dance
duty bound to be real
time regained
you are lucky
all we want
are reparations
and not revenge
our summer
should never
have been over
dear god
please put my head above my heart
i just want to crawl in bed
with a whole pie and a fork
and watch PBS
because it is quite rare
to recover shackles
from a wreck
when i see
my mom
i see god
fucking force of nature
it pains me to reflect
on my loss of purity
the erasure of black
cowboys
let me be clear
all of your black friends
if you have any
are emotionally drained
seventy-five percent
of all illnesses

are self-induced
i call this shit
post traumatic growth
you leave a little
bit of blood
in every room
vaguely seeking
material "proof"
of god, life after death, etc.
seriously think of ways
to gradually return
to the world
bats, the only mammal
capable of true flight
as blessed as i am cursed

*sweet, sweet, sweet, sweet love**

i am the vampire's wife
i wake up
every morning thinking
i know you don't love me
like you say
you do
daytime hurts my eyes
i should sit down
in the calm darkness
and have a cherry coke and a smile
i should be there for you
make the most of this
downtime
but i no longer want
to participate in this thing
called america
i want to talk more about this
but that means i need
to call out some more
people publicly
i'm not strong enough to do that yet
i can barely take care of myself
i am triggered by everything
around me
i am reminded
of everything
my ancestors lost
in the not-so-distant past
mostly, my heart
just hurts all the time
i am tired of having
to educate my white husband
i just want to scream
at the top of my lungs
all the fucking time
it's hard to see fairness
in some of the ways
the world plays out
the lack of morality
in this country is astonishing
summer of now

you leave the bones
of peter behind
hands in your pockets
while we skate
to frankie beverly
and maze
we are not northerners
but plagues
from the south
i am once again reduced
to my condolences
summer is being held over
until the sun dies

*your sympathy**

it is the year of the year
the book of job
i am poured out like water
and all my bones are out of joint
the point
is to fall in love
but at this point
i don't care
who loves me
i don't know how
to save myself
from myself
yesterday was luther's birthday
everything i've loved
i've been, or longed to be
every day the vast ocean
every headline a reminder
of how bad
the world is fucked
i listen to songs
that make me cry
so that i can cry
for the shadow i'm casting
is what's left of me
and sometimes it's like
fuck the world
and all its inhabitants
all that inhabits it
grab your lasso
of truth
assume the worst-case scenario
assume catastrophe
act accordingly
like the rock
you're clinging to
is going to smash
you to pieces
you're better off
fighting the waves
you're beautiful
but you're giving your all

to all the wrong people
and that's why
it's breaking you
i have found myself
screaming my head off
in a hotel room
i have pulled my hair out
from the root
i have stood in the water
for hours waiting
for rebirth
and for death
i have wished
for it to come
sussed out in traffic patterns
things like baptism
cooking fried apples
and how to be an american
you're the best thing
since peanut butter and jelly
dear god, please
bring her back to me

changed the plan*

baldwin refused
to hold anyone's hand
i like to be awake
before the sun is full
be fucking honest
with yourself
shit's over, whatever it was
it's gone for good
your whole world
has been redefined
i am trying to deal
with a lot of feelings rn
that have nothing
to do with you
there's someone outside
doing a side deal
with my husband
for my childhood
i, too, feel like shit
being alive
is a lie
something like the gospel
something like bedroom scripture
my only life experience
is death
suppressive heat
cicadas and someone
driving off in their pickup
with my youth
open your eyes
brother, run fast
justin bieber
with those dreadlocks
and peaches, though
the truth is a bitter pill
not a recreational drug
face it
every ugly
mocking detail
i hate the way
he chats with them

like it's his life
he's giving away
i hate the way
he's made my friends
his friends
the way he talks to b.
like he's known him for years
the way he calls n.
"norm" behind his back
there is no tender wisdom here
it is the year of being alone
i want to make sure
i'm not reinforcing
stereotypes
or profiting off black pain
at a great enough distance
we're all invisible
happy birthday to me
i am younger
than i have ever been

*guide in my pocket for fools**

how did we get here
i burn a bridge
just to prove
i'm lost
i know
the circle game
i end where i begin
i need to stop
bargaining with myself
i need to stop lying
which is worse
knowing right now
that you might not make it
or looking back
and knowing
we affixed ourselves
to a dying sea
america you is
a hypocritical nation
hard work and virtue
will not
protect you
from the tragedy
of your life
when you have
nothing left
the world
will still find
something to take
but you don't even understand
how it's so funny
cause it hurts
so much sometimes
every reason
you have
to give up
will eventually become
a memory
and a memory
is as close to nothing
as you can be

the thing that's really
transcendent
is the laugh
when it goes
in between
how you feel
you are a perpetual
outlet west
you will eventually
become
a dim memory
you're wasting
what little time
you have
to shine at all

how many times
will i let myself go
what is grief
if not preserving
love
a hole
where nobody knows
how they got there
i am exhausted by strength
i want softness
i want support
not a pat on the back
for how well i take a hit
or for how many i take
i like what you said
about clearing the grief
out of your body
if you want things
to get better
you have to stop
making them worse
i woke up this morning
and just wanted
to run and run and run
i don't know
how else to survive
i wish well-meaning people
would stop saying
i'm sorry
apologies are a courtesy
not a cure
i mean where do you put
the really heavy pain
museums are places
for dead things
to be hung
i just want to be
amongst my kin
in this summer
that does not exist
my hair is falling out
in handfuls

and i am vaping some
very mediocre vape
i come to isolation
which literally means
"to be islanded"
and i thought
that's exactly what i've been:
islanded
walking on coals
to the other side of pain
because you survived
because you are alone
because you belong
to other people
i am a diamond
i am a cancer
erasure
clinging to this one
last hunk of ice

*the rules**

it is impossible
to have ourselves
and others, too
the two of us
damage and joy
accept
there is so little
joy in here
i look at my mother's death
as a series of failures
on my part
a series of faith and
endurance on hers
i literally have
no context
for my life
without her
alice notley said
"pain swallows itself
and dies like a star"
i want you to tell me it sparkles
i want you to tell me anything
it's the middle of summer
and i have a hoodie on
seriously, fuck tokyo
i forgot my flag
and leaders
mean nothing to me
saint peter, also known as
simon or cephas
was crucified in rome
under emperor nero
according to christian tradition
i have always been
in mourning
now i worry
no one will
ever love me
erica meaning
"eternal ruler"
"ever powerful"

惠 "favor, benefit"
香 "fragrance"
梨 "pear"
i forget how sick i am
one train
hides another
all my anxiety
is separation anxiety
bodies don't last forever
you cannot save people
you can only love them
misread "comparison"
as "compassion"
you are protected
by silent friendship
you think
i cry on the outside
because that's all
you can see
parts of me died
when i sold our house
baldwin said
suffering does not isolate you
your suffering is your bridge
i guess
i, too, am a person
and can have another chance
you are alone in your one life
in your other you are free

* "it's my house"

*i'm here**

the day has passed
and gone inside
i want to have
something to say
about my own destiny
there used to be
a voice in my head
telling me everything
was going to be ok
you're not just a passenger
on a rock hurtling
through space
search for:
what does erica mean
how long is erica the game
is erica a black name
a sense of humor
as she pushed me out
into this world
don't worry
you'll find it again
everyone has to eventually
your date with god
i shouldn't leave things
so open-ended
ours is an earthbound crisis
when i think of you
i have to think of me
"you are my sunshine
my only sunshine"
i won't ever feel
warm enough
in this frightening world
everybody owes something
to everybody else
we used to make
such a good-looking couple
you are helping me just by being
genuine and real and expecting
nothing in return
questions about desire

and life's priorities
we make fake memories
to give grief some space
anything that was broken
on your journey
that strange link
between quiet and empathy
we're so very, very good
at fucking up
when i say i can walk away
i'm not fooling you
there are so many ways
to be sick

*respectfully i say to thee**

the story of the black cowboy
began when our ancestors
were brought to this country
against their will
the first kentucky derbies
were won by black jockeys
one out of four cowboys
in the west were black
every day i suddenly feel
i want to die
kanye west vh1 storytellers full show
the dark night of the soul
"positive disintegration"
"soul loss" or the "descent
to the underworld"
"nigredo" as carl jung understood it
st. john of the cross
i am not having a crisis of faith
i am having a crisis of purpose
"oscura noche"
take off my robes
and step into the choir
faith "flickers"
as illness or realization
you don't know who you really are
the so-called physical-material-industrial
plan for living
to go from emergence to emergency
sometimes i override my wiser self
and here we are
there is no logic
or feeling in loss
if you turn away
it will slowly devour you
hiraeth
a homesickness
for a place that never was
i don't think people think about me
the way that i think about them
misread
"still" as "shit"

unity is shit possible
you are a dancer
who is always really pissed
you were conditioned
assumed or habitual
that really isn't in alignment
with who you are
tireless thought
can easily burn you out
when i surrender
i am an absolute mess
to take "night" literally
would be a mistake
happiness and sadness
the rest of the world
the beginning of a way out
a black cowboy could
sit on a bull for half a day
and still not win any money

*the best**

i look like someone
healing from an accident
because i am someone
healing from an accident
the book of acts
scales falling from saul's eyes
remembering my capacity
for stillness
how long can i sit
without looking away
the fear of god escaping
i desperately need my enemies
things stay with you for a reason
warmer air
over cooler water
honestly, just call or email
if you have any questions
whatever you hear about me
please believe it
i'm sitting here
looking at ellsworth kelly paintings
and reading about
saul on the road to damascus
we are all blind sometimes
i always feel inspired
in some way
when i'm looking at art
i remember seeing duchamp
at the philly museum
and i was like, "this is it?"
seeing things up close
really puts them in perspective
a toilet bowl and broken glass
the glass organs
digressions
i believed in weight
as the right measure
people fainted and screamed
when they saw
nude descending a staircase
my heart has been burning

for so many summers now
to reckon history
and interiority
i always end up like this
leap the fence to feeling
you love all the wrong people
to stay alive

*i want the world to know**

you have to find
a place in yourself
where i am
not a part of you
or you won't be
worth loving
i know where the bodies are
the kindness that comes
after terrible enlightenment
let your warmth
be my warmth
the path of will up ahead
i want to confess
that you are me
in the moment
maybe now is not
the time to be alive
we liberate inanimate objects
what i find
i will forgive
we let go of these ghosts
let it go
and break into shards
we can start with emotion
i know you like the emotion
america makes us all sick
right now we could
all fold in half
and disappear
and you reflect
that crowded night sky
the world will hurt you
you've brought in the cold
one day the dead
will decide to stop
being dead
i'm just not in a place
to accept good things
i used to run
out to the chain of lakes
growing up means

you have to babysit
yourself
how do i stop
walking around
like i don't need anyone
the question of being here
crippled inside
i used to love the shit
out of my husband
go to heaven
in a little rowboat

*a defense that i sometimes use**

earth is ghetto
and i want to leave
no wonder
you want to look away
this year has been something else
behind those folded arms
behind that furrowed brow
your heart dissolves
i remember you
speaking of mortality
you were a flash of love
people pretending to care
attachments
cravings
we have felt in the past
we watched the last lullaby
it feels
flat-out fucking unbearable sometimes
to know you came with your friends
but who are you leaving with
i don't have any friends
i'm dreaming of what we had before
in a few years
i hope the songs
will feel like covers
surrealist max ernst said
". . . all of my hummingbirds have alibis
& 1000 profound virtues cover my body"
i agree that one is always
thinking about the right balance
last week someone fell into the ocean
so lucky i didn't fall into the ocean
some believe the house of the lord
is improvised
distills the human struggle
the trap of visibility
you look so good in yellow
skin and chest
wall structures intact
the fullness people hold
well-beyond the universe

to choose life and love
is to be temporary
you have become temporary
you become a refugee
you have been my rock
when love ends
it means someone has failed
healing also means taking
an honest look
at the role you play
in your own suffering
the patience to let go
over and over again

*like the little children**

when you say yes
you have to think
about what it's going to cost you
what is the limit on scars
they, too, need to be pretty
so we can bear looking at them
if my scars make you
feel better about yours
then i am happy
i understand you
some of us have lost
a bit of ourselves
you know there are things
you're supposed to endure
people don't trust each other
you are far more
than the sum of your mistakes
it's the last gasp of summer
and we are sweating together
i find myself at the edge often
amazed by how many edges there are
it's so hot you're hurting my feelings
what to do when hydrangeas get too big
i have no expectations from anyone
saying i love you
just hits a bit different these days
we are still birds
i want to capture something
before it's not there anymore
i go to the spa every week
i remember shampooing my mother's hair
the lather in between my fingers
her tufts of soapy grey curls
"relax" i'd say
"let me take care of you"
"i know what i'm doing"
i knew what i was doing
the existence of flowers
counting stars you never knew existed
we are older than both concepts
wildflowers, cacti, palm trees, and tall grass

you aren't just water
i thought goodness and courage would always rise
life is fun like a fucking roller coaster
you were outside once
pink and happy
and could fly over the moon

*royalties**

our hearts are in danger
when you wake up
do you think of me
my mother saw the comfort
i long to say more true things
i'll always pray to an empty sky
sea of moon
sea of maria
sea of mary
it's getting late
you were afraid of yourself
i tried to tell you
there are so many reasons to cry
i'm not poet enough
to address this feeling
i try to wear the world
like it is some kind of comet
to open and depart it
to be a body
this is the end of love
we're not in this together
we just happen
to be walking the same way
i can show myself out
don't come to me for distance
i thought i was going home
i want us to be more sincerely thoughtful
about how we take from people
we do not care about
getting a seat at the table used to be the goal
now we all see that the table sucks
we need to build new tables
have mercy
those answers don't matter anymore
and they are selfish questions in the first place
guilt is about us
fields of forgetful time
every few weeks my life burns down
regal branches against a night sky
a garden of ice
a glass full of glass
it is the end of summer and i need you

* *"my old piano"*

*i'm doing ok**

i forget how things really used to be
in reality we are all monsters
i believe that death looks like
what i see in my dreams
a black hole where you get to be
with everyone you miss
i ate a peach today
you called them "bathtub peaches"
because you had to lean over one to eat them
to catch the juice
i've never had a peach taste so good
what if i am holding on too tightly to life
i am not afraid of not having feelings
we believe no one ever notices our suffering
maybe you were the ocean when i was a stone
maybe you just learn lessons better than me then
being someone's child somehow forces you
to accept your emotional inadequacy
how i express that love towards you
sometimes the relationship dictates that you separate
we always come back to the song we were singing
i'm so sorry you're going through so much
you deserve the world
go to every hot spring & hold your breath underwater
every time you come up it will be a new world
you think i have what you want
you think i won't give it to you
waves are washing me out
i am crying over everyone's tears
a ton of dumplings
watching reruns of the american music awards
you grab the snoopy comics from my room
you thought you were doing me a favor
to rearrange time
while you gather its energy
i'd like to remember my mother's smile
we continually come back to see things
we thought we understood
you will become your greatest strength
i have kept this from you
i feel like we both should listen

to some prince right now
because i would die for you

*i'm no great pretender**

if you can read this, you are alive
you're going to get your ass kicked
whether you're afraid or not
we recite ourselves to life
remember that in your moments
of grief or uncertainty
the body in contact with darkness
you must return to what birthed you
when the body rests, it heals
black people in the hands of black people
an algorithm
became willing to see myself
refused to be knowable
would not believe the lie of permanence
you left me
holding the bowl of honey
i can picture you in my arms right now
let time happen
step over the gravestone
walk the periphery
watched them put her in the ground
to see the world again
thought i could know the world
you don't know what hurt is
to let myself be alive
your presence was no longer my burden
my body this last winter
perpetual reconciliation
you want to pull away now
everything is burning down around you
do not be afraid to disappear
be naked
call me a lioness
the path isn't a straight line
being an only child teaches you
to apologize for every time i wasn't there
i swear like a sailor at the drop of a hat
stay conscious of the apparatus
your hollows
composure
when we are separate and alone

what if what i want from you isn't new
savagery is genetic
i'm sitting in my mother's house
wine drunk in the middle of her bed
wearing her mink coat, crying
i could kill right now
i can't die
any slower

look at me
can't even spell love
what a mess
going through motions
to go viral and not find shelter
i want to stop attracting people with problems
problems that at some point i will be called upon
in some capacity to fix
now i'm thinking about touching you
inviting you to my studio instead of tea at a café
i want to bite your lip
and pull your body
into mine
how it's hard enough to survive and then survive again
they keep killing black people and i need the wifi password
how to leave your husband
how i did not make love to you
i try to resolve things but you don't want to be sorry
we could have the one thing or everything
a clumsy metaphor for my faculties
just stop the fucking things
just stop
triggered by something that has absolutely nothing to do with you
we enjoy each other
we are breathing through it
i think the lone ranger called his horse trigger
go on
teach me a lesson
what would you really miss if everything burned
i have built a home with another person
never expecting it to last
the hollow feeling of unwanted beginnings
my own awareness of love
the intimacy of answering the phone
your voice thick with sleep
shared hesitancy
text me when you're home safe
wanted to reveal silence
because this made me think of you

what we know is true
there will come a time when you experience a sorrow so deep
you may find yourself clinging to the floor
choking on your own tears
this fierceness is also beautiful
categories of pain
a weepy day for both of us
it is a grace nonetheless
living in the house of better
words we can't pronounce
money for clothes
remembrances
the basis of need to know
when you take a deep breath
i feel like dropping things
whales so close you can touch them
drownings on a subway
every day i die over and over again
in this life you were meant to fail
'80s saxophone solo
something moves when you take a deep breath
this is also rest
it's always been about me
began to see that there are consequences
your tears are a testament of the deep
love that you shared
i've never liked this side of me
i'm different than i remember
i want to stand up
but i'm out of breath
out of practice
it feels like versailles now
we normally start in the dark
we start with the letters
passion to cover my flaws
vaccinated but afraid to go out again
honesty is better when it's practiced
some things will push you forward and then let you go
no more sidewalk
to prove you are real

participation medal
some of you is missing
every time i watch the news i delete pieces of myself
i am super grateful to have known you
that you will not be owned by fear
observed the flowers someone left for her
love by itself isn't always enough
the pendulum will always keep shifting
you are worth everything you desire
it's that each day you try to forget the massive thing
try to live with the small
ask why am i like this
i don't know any better
takes death and trash and doesn't remember
i mean can i take these away from you
stands in front of me ready to suggest
i have ways of passing
of straight faces that fool everyone
what rides us hard
because there is nothing worse
even now
nothing else to do but back up
into myself
burst and fade

*i feel so brokenhearted**

the lord is helping me in small and important ways
watches the ysl show
runs herself through the wringer
there are two kinds of forgetting
an infinity of dead before me
flowers grow out of my grave
things change around you
you rest in the inevitability of things
ignore your desire
stop suffering
give away your possessions
came down from that cloud
america makes us all artists
sees migrants as modern slaves
lies about instinct
because blood doesn't lie
we are all combustible
what if i stopped and just sat with who & what i am
walk through the doors that are
say this is a good day to take some deep breaths & remember love
i think about you often
all i want to do is be together
i've been depending on the overgrown
something else i want to leave you with
in the deep dark horror trenches of healing
i choose you again
some people never let you go
empathy becomes expensive when you have empathy for everyone
but yourself
i want to be loved as a choice not as a reward
sometimes the best choice is the one that's the easiest to live with
maybe you just learn lessons
i can't remember the last time something wasn't going to shit
long summer days
if i never get well
i am looking at the fucking sun
sometimes the universe
all my whiskey
this is the way to remember
i miss you
i'll be there after while

we live in a perpetually burning building
i felt only softness
my open wounds
having no place
i'm on my way home
everybody say glory

acknowledgments

Portions of *mahogany* appeared in the following publications: *Yale Review, American Poetry Review, The Brooklyn Rail, Gasher, Guest, Sink, Sporklet, The Tiny, Weekly Gramma.*

"ain't that easy" aired on WFMT Radio Network as part of the Poetry Foundation series, *PoetryNow.*

Portions of part one appeared as a chapbook entitled *teak* from Afterhours Editions / The Song Cave.

Many thanks to those editors for their support.

Infinite gratitude: Cindy Arrieu-King, Sommer Browning, Mark Finein

Thank you: Natalie Brown; Cody Caronna; Norman Finklestein; Callie Floor; Emily Kedall Frey; Sheryl Mobley Brown; Rebecca Moses; Tyrone Williams; Jessica Yohn

project notes

One of the strongest things you can do is bear witness.

This book was written during the years I care gave for my mother, Mary. Her long illness was the best and worst time in my life. For five years I shuffled between San Francisco and Cincinnati, six months by six months. We had a mother-daughter relationship that transcended being parent and child. She was my light, my protector, my cheerleader, my conscience, my best friend. My everything. It was not only my duty but my absolute pleasure to care for her in her final years as she had cared for me my entire life: with strength, humor, and love.

Diana Ross was a staple in our household. We listened to her oldies with The Supremes and her solo albums and watched *The Wiz* whenever local TV aired it. When I discovered *Lady Sings the Blues*, I swooned and cried. *Mahogany* showed me how absolutely beautiful we were and could be. Our style, strength, and blackness were not accidents, nor were they undesirable.

mahogany is the last book in the "box set" trilogy. Like the first two books, *daryl hall is my boyfriend* and *mary wants to be a superwoman*, *mahogany* uses the music of a (once popular) pop artist that I grew up listening to. Each poem takes its title from a line of a Diana Ross and The Supremes song or a song from Diana's successful solo career—the poems are not "about" the actual songs, but what is triggered when listening to or thinking about the music. I'm thinking about what happens when you take something like a pop song and turn it in on itself, give it a different frame of reference, juxtapose the work against itself, against other pop music, and bring it into the present.

Within contemporary poetry I am invested in merging the historical and the beloved through reverence for my roots, my family, music, and pop culture: the things we actually live with and among. The entire "box set" trilogy is my take on revising the confessional, but whereas *daryl hall* focuses on memory and childhood and nostalgia, and *mary* delves more factually into my family history and how to live and move on from that history and its implications, *mahogany* is a story about the passing of time and unimaginable loss, trying to find a little joy amidst a lot of chaos. The dailiness of finding that joy.

about the author

erica lewis lives in San Francisco where she runs lil' homie apothecary. Her books include the "box set" trilogy (*daryl hall is my boyfriend, mary wants to be a superwoman, mahogany*); *all the real tears; murmur in the inventory;* and *camera obscura* and *precipice of jupiter,* with artist Mark Stephen Finein. Her work has appeared in various anthologies and journals and in numerous chapbooks. She was born in Cincinnati, Ohio.